MATTERS OF PROPORTION

THE RESIDENCE OF RICHARD KOEHLER ~ N·W· 19TH AVENUE & JOHNSON STREET ~ 1905

RICHARD MARLITT

MATTERS OF PROPORTION

The Portland Residential Architecture of Whidden & Lewis

RICHARD MARLITT

OREGON HISTORICAL SOCIETY PRESS

COVER ILLUSTRATION: *The Henry Edwards Residence, drawing by Richard Marlitt.*

FRONTIS: *The Richard Koehler Residence, drawing by Richard Marlitt.*

Designed and produced by the Oregon Historical Society Press.

The paper used in this publication meets the minimum requirements of American National Standard for Information Sciences—Permanence of Paper for Printed Library Materials, ANSI Z39.48-1984.

Library of Congress Cataloging-in-Publication Data

Marlitt, Richard, 1909-
    Matters of Proportion: the Portland residential
    architecture of Whidden and Lewis / Richard Marlitt.
    p.   cm.
    1. Architecture, Domestic—Oregon—Portland.   2.
    Portland (Or.)—Buildings, structures, etc.   I.
    Whidden and Lewis.   II. Title.
    NA7238.P575M37   1989
    728'.37'0922—dc20   89-9325
    ISBN 0-87595-177-5   CIP

Printed in the United States of America.

CONTENTS

MATTERS OF PROPORTION

PROLOGUE

WHEN I WAS A SMALL BOY I liked to look at houses, and now after half a century it is still a favorite pastime. As a youngster, however, I kept my interest in architecture a secret; nonconformity was not admired on the playground. How unfortunate I did not reveal my secret to some doting aunt or uncle who might have given me a camera. If they had, this volume would be a treasury of Portland architecture. I knew the mansions along King Avenue and had favorites spotted all through the area north of Burnside Street, which at that time was called Nob Hill. But I was not the only one who missed the opportunity to photograph these houses. Then, as now, people took pictures of one another, of rivers and mountains, and even of their dogs. Yet they showed a strange reluctance to photograph their dwelling places. This shows keenly in the meager photograph files of residential work at the Oregon Historical Society. A good deal of blame can be laid on the architects, who relegate residential design low on their list of priorities because it involves a great deal of work for a nominal return. Even such nationally known architects as Stanford White and John Russell Pope, when publishing, seldom promoted their handsome houses ahead of their public buildings.

William Whidden and Ion Lewis, who formed the prestigious Portland architectural firm of Whidden and Lewis, were guilty of the same crime. I have wanted for many years to assemble their fine houses in a manuscript, but when I started the task I was amazed at how little there was from which to work. I wanted views of the houses that I remembered as a small boy, but they simply are not available.

I remember every morning walking up Nineteenth Avenue to school and passing a Whidden and Lewis house with great bay windows to the street. Five mornings a week a family sat around the table in full view,

Valuable artwork and beautiful furnishings filled the living room of the Henry Jagger Corbett house.

Like the other rooms in the Henry Jagger Corbett house, the master bedroom had a look of great comfort.

The cabinet work and the ceiling cove in the dining room of the Frank Warren house are examples of fine craftsmanship.

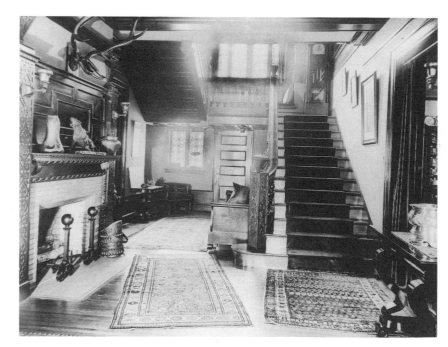

The Frank Warren house featured a wealth of fine mill work, cornices, paneling, and carving.

having their breakfast served. The lower part of the house was done in tawny rough brick and the upper part in redwood shingles. What I would give for a photograph!

My wife's grandmother lived as a widow in one of Whidden and Lewis' large country houses looking out over the Willamette River in what has become Dunthorpe. There were deep porches and a lawn sweeping down to the river bluff, where a little steam train ran to Oswego. Not a soul in that large family took a picture of the place. On my daily walk to the old Lincoln High School I passed a beautiful Colonial house at Tenth Avenue and Clay Street; it was as handsome a house as Whidden and Lewis had designed. In the summertime bamboo chairs would be set out on the circular terrace that jutted out from the front of the house, shaded by a striped awning. The Ladd family built the house and gave it to the Portland Academy for the headmaster, but even the school did not bother to photograph it. It is no wonder that collecting material for this book has been a task.

But back to my early fondness for looking at houses. I could not see these houses without wanting to know more about the people who built them. I was not old enough to know that theirs was a generation that was reaping the rewards of a town that just recently had grown enough to be a city. The overalls had been laid aside and the covered wagon burned. No longer was there an aching desolation of three-thousand miles between loved ones and civilized ways. Portland had arrived. A railroad ran across the plains, through the Rockies, and down the Columbia River Gorge. Comfortable passenger steamers sailed to San Francisco, and there was macadam paving on the downtown streets. There were fine cast-iron buildings along those streets fronting the river, which was spanned to the east side by two bridges. It was a time to enjoy the fruits of labor, to enjoy "gracious living" (a description that curiously has returned to dominate many real estate ads today). Gracious living was not hard to achieve, as Portland at the end of the nineteenth century had taken on a sleek sophistication. The city had an art museum, the beginnings of a symphony, good theater, a fine library, and a social life augmented by new fortunes and New England backgrounds.

Accommodations were needed for this style of living, and fine houses started to rise against the west hills and on the east side of the river. How they lived in those houses! Heavy velvet draperies were drawn at night and sometimes during the day for elaborate luncheons. Fine china and crystal adorned the tables for enormous dinners that went on course after course. Irish maids lived on the top floors, and a Chinese cook had quarters in the basement. Ladies wore Parisian dresses for afternoon calls, when they always left their cards on a silver tray in the hall. Calls were made in smart turnouts with a coachman, and in later years the coachman became the driver of a Lozier, a Locomobile, or—the epitome of high style—a Pierce Arrow. A golf club was created beyond Sellwood, one of the first in the West. The children went to St. Helen's Hall, the oldest Episcopalian school west of the Rockies, or to the Portland Academy, housed in one of Whidden and Lewis' finest buildings (which not long ago was replaced by a section of freeway).

As a boy watching all this, I could not realize that I was seeing a manner of living that would falter with the

First World War and finally succumb during the Depression. Nor could I know that the grand houses of the time would not survive as such. The tentacles of the business district surrounded many of them, and they became rooming houses and then were demolished. Others, by a quirk of geography, were located in neighborhoods that remained unmarred, and they were used for institutional offices or turned into apartments. Only seven of the fifty houses listed in this book still are private homes—and very beautiful ones, I might add.

This entire period lasted two generations, and then it was gone. The Sevres china and the Aubusson rugs brought back from the grand tour abroad went to the smaller homes of children, as did Oriental objects picked up in Chinatown that now are considered priceless. The paintings of Childe Hassam and Alden Weir found their way into the Oregon Art Institute, along with the French Impressionist works, which were considered strange at that time but are the pride of our museum today. I still like looking at those great houses I enjoyed as a boy, but now I see them as more than examples of fine architecture. They sheltered strong individuals who sank their stakes deeply into this golden city they learned to love. They left Portland a strong character and an ageless elegance that has lasted over the years, though the elm-shaded streets are gone and the sternwheeler *Hassalo* no longer takes us to summers at the beach.

INTRODUCTION

THE YEAR was 1888, and in Portland a high board fence had been erected along the west side of Sixth Avenue from Morrison to Yamhill streets to hide a weathered foundation and a yawning excavation. Six years earlier, Henry Villard had brought the Northern Pacific Railroad into Portland, generating a need for hotel facilities. Villard had commissioned the East Coast architectural firm of McKim, Mead and White to design a hotel for the Morrison-Yamhill block, and a young man named William Marcy Whidden was selected to be the resident architect representing the firm. During the financial panic of 1883, however, all work on the hotel was halted. Tired of looking at "Villard's Ruins," a group of Portland citizens formed a corporation in 1888, bought the property, and asked Charles McKim to proceed with the plans. By that time, however, McKim had lost interest in the hotel, and the job was offered to Whidden, who purchased the commission. Whidden realized that in coming to Portland he would have to form his own office, and that the move would be a permanent one. Many of his ties with the East would be severed.

William Whidden was born in Boston in 1857. He graduated from Boston Tech, which we now know as the Massachusetts Institute of Technology, and then spent four years in Paris acquiring a fine architectural background. Ion Lewis also was a Bostonian, born in the suburb of Lynn in 1853, and he also had graduated from Boston Tech. Whidden and Lewis had known one another in eastern architectural offices. Lewis' training came from the Boston office of Peabody and Stearns, which was as well known nationally as McKim, Mead and White. In 1889 he visited Portland and renewed his friendship with Whidden, who had just established his office. Whidden, realizing that he probably would need a partner—preferably one with a background similar to his own—asked Lewis if he would consider the job. It would be interesting to know how much persuasion was required to convince Lewis to stay in Portland. The old saying, "Go west, young

Comfort was not an issue in the early Whidden and Lewis offices, and the lighting was medieval. Under the skylight around the drafting boards are, from left to right, Ion Lewis, William Whidden, Albert E. Doyle, and Seth Catlin. Albert Doyle later formed his own practice and designed many of Portland's important buildings.

man" was still popular, and Portland, a bit of New England transplanted to the Pacific Northwest, could have held a special appeal. In any event, Lewis was convinced, and in 1889 the two young men set up the first bona fide architectural office in the city.

Previously, architecture in Portland had not seen such polished ability and as great a volume of work. The hotel that instigated the partnership was an immediate success. Built of brick and stone in the Queen Anne style, "The Portland" was as fine a hostelry as any in the West. For sixty years it reigned as the social center of the city, until sadly, in the name of "progress," it became a parking lot. After the hotel was built, commissions rolled in, and many of those projects became the best known buildings in the city: the City Hall, the Multnomah County Court House, the original part of the Good Samaritan Hospital, and numerous office buildings and houses. This monograph focuses only on the residential work of Whidden and Lewis and gives it the credit it deserves. The houses designed by the firm represent an originality of styling, fine proportions, taste, and the excellence of design that they put into each project.

Both men left behind their eastern connections and settled into the Portland scene. William Whidden married Alice Wygant, great granddaughter of Dr. John McLoughlin, a founding father of Oregon. The Whiddens and their family of twin boys occupied a handsome country house above the river at Rivera. Ion Lewis remained a bachelor and lived out his years at the Arlington Club. Around 1892 Charles Ladd built the Concord Building at the corner of Southwest Second Avenue and Stark Street for the offices of the Portland Flouring Mills and for Balfour, Guthrie, and Company, the British milling house. Whidden and Lewis designed that building, and the sixth floor housed their offices for many years.

When Whidden died in 1929, Lewis continued the firm's work at their last offices in the Wilcox Building. His death in 1933 ended an architectural practice that spanned nearly forty-five years. These were years of great change in the West, as in the entire nation, but the work of Whidden and Lewis carried a stamp of consistency through those years, bringing tasteful design from the chaos of the Victorian era.

MATTERS OF PROPORTION

THE COLONIAL REVIVAL: A RETURN TO SANITY

STUDYING BOOKS written on the history of architecture, one finds few discussions on anything but religious and public buildings. Mentioned first are the tombs of the Egyptian Pharaohs, followed by the Greek temples of the Acropolis. From there the Classical order is passed down to the Roman forums, the vast baths, and again the temples. The Gothic period of Europe is a study of the cathedral, its form and construction. It was not until the Renaissance that attention was given to man's shelter—but even that was in the form of vast Italian palazzi and villas, great French chateaux and palaces, and magnificent English manor houses. Although these structures conceded that a residence no longer had to be a place of defense, they still could hardly be considered common dwellings. Not until the mid-eighteenth century in England was the single dwelling of a middle-class family deserving of any architectural merit.

America had been settled by that time and was predominantly an agricultural society for which the single-family residence was appropriate. The new colonies were British, and it was only natural that the craftsmen of the early eighteenth century turned to the mother country for inspiration. The fine houses of Charleston, Philadelphia, Boston, and Salem were derived from Georgian models of the old country, although on a modest scale. Lacking the wealth of England, American craftsmen created what came to be known as the Colonial style, a simple, well-proportioned structure embellished with good detailing. The Colonial style gave the impression of comfortable living—as comfortable as could be had at that time. At last there was a domestic form of architecture that could be included in historical studies, a single-unit building created for the great middle class who neither could afford nor cared to live in a palace like Versailles, a Hampton Court, or a Villa D'Este. Middle class residential architecture was to evolve through variations of this style, echoing the national taste (or lack of it)—variations that at times were plagiarized from the past and at other times showed the development of something fresh and new.

   The office of McKim, Mead and White (where Whidden got his start) and that of Peabody and Stearns (which employed Lewis) were the top-flight disciples of the domestic work that was being created in Boston, New York, and neighboring areas. At McKim, Mead and White there was a concurrent expansiveness of design that historians called an academic imitation; it was a revival of eighteenth-century forms and a reaction against the Victorian picturesque. That office was the first to return to this extreme formal order. An excellent example of this is the residence of H. A. C. Taylor in Newport, Rhode Island (opposite page 3), designed by McKim, Mead and White in 1885. There is the symmetrical Anglo-Palladian plan of the mid-eighteenth century with the center hall, rooms of equal width on either side, and balanced appendages beyond the main mass. The exterior is a rectangular block with balancing ornamented windows rising to a hip roof (although a gable-end roof could be substituted), dominant dormers for good third-floor light, and heavy, evenly placed chimneys. The detailing is of a Georgian order, and the whole effect is one of dignity and simplicity. This house provided a new formula of design for domestic work that superseded the picturesque Victorian houses of a few years earlier. Here McKim, Mead and White started the Colonial Revival, which was to last longer than any domestic style in America before it. The way in which Whidden and Lewis adapted this style to their own use is the basis of the first chapter.

The Lucien W. Wallace Residence
Northwest Flanders Street at
the corner of Twenty-Fourth Avenue

IN THIS HANDSOME HOUSE one can see at once the effect that their East Coast training had on both Whidden and Lewis. The house also shows the influence that the Taylor residence had on design. The balanced division of windows around the entrance porch, the narrow shutters, and the Palladian window heads are almost duplicated from the Taylor house. There is the same wide cornice board under the eaves to give the facade necessary height, and there are the same important dormers. Even the hip roof is topped with a railing. The broad terrace across the front provides an essential horizontal line. The entire mass is beautifully proportioned and almost perfect in scale. Portland was little more than forty years old when this house was created in 1888-89, one of Whidden and Lewis' first residential ventures. The place was a credit to the taste of the new city's residents.

Lucien Wallace died in 1890, having lived only a year in the house. It was sold in 1891 to Charles Plummer, the Portland head of the W. P. Fuller Company. The Plummers lived there until 1908, when George W. Bates purchased the property. Bates asked Whidden and Lewis to completely remodel the exterior. A great porch was built across the front with columns that did not match the existing ones, and the delightful little orangery was removed. A porch with Corinthian columns was added to the second floor, and three heavy dormers replaced the originals. The architects' approach to the remodeling is puzzling; they lost all the domestic quality of the original house and instead achieved a top-heavy design without character.

The Bates family and then the Frederick Seller family lived in the house for many years. It has been divided into apartments and is still beautifully cared for.

5

The Judge Charles B. Bellinger Residence
The block of Northeast Holladay Street, Grand Avenue, Sixth Avenue, and Hassalo Street

A PLEASANT PORTLAND MEMORY is Holladay Street in the 1920s and 1930s. Great New England elms shaded the street for blocks, providing a beautiful setting for the fine houses that lined the street. In fact, the initial planting of elms shows in this photograph of the Bellinger residence.

Charles Bellinger was a judge of the United States District Court. In 1890 he commissioned Whidden and Lewis to design this house. It was one of the many fine residences built in the Holladay Addition and was a complete turnabout from the Victorian houses shown in the background of the photograph. The basic elements of the Taylor house were used once again: a balanced facade consisting of a central entrance porch with equal windows on either side, and one-story appendages on each end of the main mass. The railed front terrace, important dormers, and massive chimneys complete the design. This property and the rest of the area was taken for the development of the Lloyd Center.

The William L. Brewster Residence
Northwest Lovejoy Street between Twenty-Fourth and Twenty-Fifth avenues

THE CLEAN, SIMPLE LINES of this house give it an attractive air. Again, the architects used a center entrance, this time with a portico porch that echoes the dentil course under the cornice. Actually, the only other detailing is the interesting porch railing. The houses throughout this chapter are examples of the ways in which Whidden and Lewis attempted to make the third floor livable. In this case, however, they raised the cornice so high for head room that the whole facade seems top-heavy; the over-sized dormer spoils the proportions of the facade.

The hill in the background is the site of old St.

Vincent Hospital. The area's wooden sidewalks and dirt streets must have been trying during the winter.

The Russell Hubbard Residence
Northwest Twentieth Avenue at
the corner of Irving Street

THE HUBBARD FAMILY occupied this comfortable, substantial house for more than sixty years. They must have enjoyed the large windows lighting the rooms and the long covered porch with the decorative railing at the second floor; a front porch was particularly pleasant at that time, when street traffic was at a minimum. Unlike the single dormer on the Brewster house, the one on the Hubbard house fits nicely into the composition of the facade.

Unfortunately, this simple, timeless residence is gone now, the land occupied by an apartment complex.

The Theodore Brooks Trevett Residence
2347 Northwest Flanders Street

THIS HOUSE was erected in 1891, at a time when many architects still clung to Victorian frills; yet its design is almost stark in its simplicity. Changes in taste were slow coming west, but the arrival of Whidden and Lewis from Boston heralded a new frugality in design that appealed to Portland. Here, the simple facade is broken only by large bay windows facing south. It is interesting to compare this facade with that of the Holt Wilson house, which was also designed in the early 1890s. The high eave line, which created a somewhat top-heavy effect, was used in both designs, as were the bay windows. There is a playful bit of architecture in the oval windows of the side dormer encasing the chimney. The house has been painted an ivory color with dark green shutters, and the second-floor porch railing has been replaced. It is still a dignified, ageless residence.

Theodore Trevett's wife, Mary, was the daughter of Azariah Bancroft, the Indian agent at Fort Simcoe near Yakima, Washington. When Mary and Theodore were married, they moved to Portland and built this house. Later, when their daughter Emily married Dr. Richard K. Nunn, the Trevetts gave them the house. Richard Nunn had been a doctor in the Wexford Irish Militia, and during the First World War he served in the United States Medical Corps. Emily Nunn and her sister Lucy were pioneers among Portland women who devoted themselves to social betterment causes. They were very involved with the Womens International League for Peace and Freedom and the Consumers League for Betterment of Working Conditions. The Nunn home, as the residence became known, served as a meeting place for many of their activities and causes and also became a salon for the artistic, bohemian, and literary circles of Portland.

The Edward A. King Residence
Southwest King Avenue at Yamhill Street

NAHUM KING was an Oregon pioneer whose land claim became part of the city's expanion. The claim stretched from West Burnside Street to Jefferson Street and from approximately Southwest Fourteenth Avenue westward beyond Washington Park. The King homestead was near the northwest corner of the present Multnomah Stadium. As the city grew and the land became more valuable, King platted it into building sites, and the area became a very fashionable neighborhood. The land rose gently from Tanners Creek up into the Portland Heights, affording most residences a sweeping view of the city and the Cascade Range.

In 1912 Nahum King commissioned Whidden and Lewis to design this house for his son Edward. It is a Colonial Revival design with a center hall. A dining room and kitchen are to the left of the entrance, and the living room is to the right, with a library behind it. Like other houses on King Avenue, this one has a porch that stretches across the back to take advantage of the view. With this plan and the simple exterior lines, it was an excellent piece of domestic work.

After Edward King died, the Frank E. Watkins family lived here for many years. A few years ago the house's facade was altered, but the place is still standing.

The Judge Wallace McCamant Residence

Southwest King Avenue between
Salmon and Main streets

THE PROTOTYPE for this classic town house can be found along the elm-lined streets of Boston, Salem, or Newburyport, Massachusetts, where the three-story facade flourished in another attempt to give third-floor bedrooms full-height ceilings. This house has an unusual floor plan. A large hall housing a very handsome staircase takes up all the space to the right of the entrance. The living room and dining room are along the rear of the house, opening onto a long covered porch. When the house was built, it had a fine view of the city, but that long since has been blocked by apartment buildings. Originally, the windows were undivided with a single sash, and the house was painted a deep tan with brown trim and black shutters, very typical of the 1890s. It is still a family home and is in excellent condition.

The William R. MacKenzie Residence

1131 Southwest King Avenue

THIS HANDSOME HOUSE faces the McCament residence on King Avenue and mirrors it with the same three-story facade. The floor plan, however, is quite different. A center hall runs through to the rear of the house with a living room on one side and a dining room on the other. Both of these rooms are quite narrow, but Whidden and Lewis attempted to widen them with bay windows. The two-story addition that shows in the photograph replaced a pleasant porch that once looked across the canyon to the Portland Heights.

The Robert Farrell family lived in the house for many years, and it is still a private residence.

The Henry Edwards Residence
Southwest Main Street at
the corner of St. Clair Avenue

KING HILL AROUND 1910 must have been a very beautiful neighborhood, with grand residences of the same size and caliber grouped around St. Helen's Hall. But although their owners were prosperous, the houses were doomed. Taxes and unwieldy size hastened their downfall.

In this dignified design, Whidden and Lewis used another approach to gain head room for the third floor. They placed a cornice and gutter at the normal height above the second-story windows, then added a wide facia, before the roof slope begins. Dormers were brought out to this facia, giving the impression of size and dominance. These variations appear again in the Max M. Lang house, which backs against this one, and in the Isam White residence. These houses, built around the same time, share other interesting similarities as well. Each has a vestibule at the front entrance that opens into a large hall stretching across two-thirds of the front; the hall houses a fireplace and a very dominant stairway. The remaining part of the front is the living room or, in the White residence, the dining room. The Edwards and the Lang homes have carriage entrances from St. Clair Avenue, and all three houses have the usual side entrance porch with open terraces on either side.

Henry Edwards founded a large retail furniture outlet that lasted until after the Second World War. He sold this house, after occupying it only a few years, to Julius Steinbach, whose name became attached to it. Today it is occupied by offices, but it has retained its residential character. If you can envision the original dark green shutters at the windows and turned balusters on the terrace, you will agree that it is a very successful piece of design.

11

The James D. Honeyman Residence
Southwest St. Clair Avenue at Park Place

THERE ARE INFINITE WAYS to design the facade of a house with a center hall. In the Honeyman residence, Whidden and Lewis took a new tack: The front door was placed in a bay extending to the roof cornice, and large plate glass windows were used. The design succeeds on most levels, although the broken pediment and the paneling of the dormer were a bit heavy in light of the delicate railing above the porch and the fine facia board and dentil course under the eaves, which actually are a double row of dentils.

James Honeyman and his brothers owned the Honeyman Hardware Company, probably the largest hardware outlet in Oregon at the time. James' house backs against brother William's on King Avenue (discussed in a later chapter). Though this is a very old picture, the era of the automobile had arrived when it was taken; the garage had been placed as far from the house as possible, and the hitching post was retained—just in case.

Just before the First World War the house was drastically remodeled by David Lewis. Lewis, a member of the Couch family, had been trained at Princeton and was an excellent architect. People often switch architects without reason, but in this case David Lewis was chosen because of his connections to the family; Mrs. Lewis was James Honeyman's sister. Lewis chose to elongate the front, adding to the left side of the house. The front door was moved to the left, to center it on the new facade. The terrace railing and the handsome cornice remain; the railing over the front porch was present after the remodeling, but it disappeared years ago. Envision dark shutters at the windows and ignore the tall apartment house next door frowning down on you, and you still have a beautiful town house.

12

The Winslow B. Ayer Residence
1808 Northwest Johnson Street

WHIDDEN AND LEWIS designed two houses for W. B. Ayer, the president of the Eastern and Western Lumber Company. He was a sympathetic, highly cultured client, and perhaps that is what made both houses so successful architecturally. Ayer was a New Englander who came to Portland to join the J. K. Gill Company. He moved on to wealth and civic stature as one of the Northwest's leading lumbermen.

This house soundly represents the return to historical precedence that had been made by such Eastern architectural firms as Shepley, Rutan and Coolidge; McKim, Mead and White; and Carrere and Hastings. Whidden and Lewis put as much purity and beauty into the facade as their eastern predecessors could have. Surprisingly, the innovations here, such as the circular portico at the entrance repeated with handsome curved bays on either side, were not used again. The first-floor windows featured high Palladian heads that were not repeated on the second floor.

For many years the John Francis Shea family occupied the house, and later the John London family of Balfour, Guthrie and Company lived there. It is now divided into apartments, but the facade is quite the same.

The J. Frank Watson Residence
Southwest Park Avenue at the corner of Hall Street

BEFORE THE ADVENT of Portland State University, the west side of the Park Blocks was lined with large houses, each of which occupied at least a half block. Most of them were more ornate than the Watson residence, although its front porch did at one time have an intricate railing over the entrance that returned to the pilasters on either side of the second-floor door. A fine effect is lost without it. The off-centered front door is a design that Whidden and Lewis used several times. They also used gambrel roofs

on many of their houses; it was a good design for making the third floor usable. Through the front door one entered a vestibule that led into the large hall; a nook with a seat took up the remainder of the space in the center. The house was built for a generation that liked nooks and corners, but a straight-forward approach would have made a more pleasing design overall. The covered driveway is one feature that more Portland houses should have. How nice to arrive under cover during one of our winter downpours!

Originally from New England, Joseph Frank Watson was the president of the Merchants National Bank and a partner in the Smith and Watson Iron Works. John Whalley, a noted Portland barrister, was his father-in-law. The Whalley home, a great Victorian pile, stood next to the Watson home. Both were demolished to make way for Portland State University.

The James M. Russell Residence
1135 Southwest Vista Avenue

THE SIDE VIEW of the Watson residence (shown previously) clearly indicates just how enormous some of these houses were. The Russell house is a more manageable size, and perhaps that is why it has been maintained as a private residence. The house was not always on busy Vista Avenue. Vista, once called Ford Street, came to a dead end in front of this house, and not until years later when a car line was needed to Portland Heights was a bridge built across the canyon. Privacy was gone forever.

This house has a typical center-hall plan, but the usual terrace across the front was omitted; instead there is a terrace on the south side, which has a view of the Heights. The hip roof and simple dormers give a low-keyed effect, and the corner quoins are interesting to note; usually done in stone, Whidden and Lewis executed them beautifully in wood; now they are painted to match the trim.

14

The Dr. Lauritz W. Therkelsen Residence

*Southwest Eleventh Avenue at
the corner of Market Street*

THIS LARGE HOUSE, with its high gambrel roof, stood very close to the street and was every bit as overpowering as it looks in the photograph. In its last years it was used for institutional offices, which seems to be more in its character than its original use as a home. An 1882 panorama of the city shows a very large Victorian house on this site. Dr. Therkelsen had Whidden and Lewis either move it or remodel it into the house we see in the picture.

For most of its residential life this was the home of the Ladd and Tilton banker Edward Cookingham and his family. Like most of the houses in the neighborhood, it succumbed to Portland State University.

The Isam White Residence

Northwest Twentieth Avenue at Everett Street

EIGHT OR TEN of the houses Whidden and Lewis designed fall into the category of mansions. This one, built in 1905, is certainly one of them. It has changed little over the years although the original light exterior color scheme made it easier to appreciate the fine detailing. The exterior is a balanced Colonial facade with the centered entrance, balustraded terrace, and matching side wings, which in this case are small porches behind Palladian arches. The heavy Corinthian pilasters at the corners support a cornice with a raised roof and dormers. The area between the raised roof and the cornice is carried over the side wings with a baluster railing, which continues over the pleasant rounded bay on the Everett Street side.

Again, a vestibule opens into a great hall that stretches part way across the front of the house. The hall is paneled in hardwood with Doric pi-

15

lasters that support a heavy frieze, and it houses a large fireplace at one end. An elaborate staircase is at the rear, with a fine stained-glass window at the landing. The effect is quite the same as that of the great hall in the Zera Snow house; both were among the finest rooms in the city at the time. To the right of the entrance is the dining room, and behind that on the Everett Street side is an oval morning room. A paneled library is at the rear corner.

Isam White and his brother Levi came from Germany and became very successful importers in Portland. As a child, Mrs. White started at the St. Mary's Academy when the nuns first arrived from Montreal. She was one of the school's earliest graduates.

The Max M. Lang Residence
2188 Southwest Park Place

THIS HOUSE, the Edwards house behind it, and the Isam White house all were built in 1904 and 1905 and are very similar in plan, yet each seems to maintain its own individuality. In the Lang house, a vestibule at the front door opens into a great hall that takes up two-thirds of the front of the house; the Langs used this for a sitting room. A baronial staircase rises from the hall, and there is a fireplace at the west end. The windows to the left of the front door light a room that has such a formal air it can only be called a drawing room. This room and the dining room behind it still have the original tapestry cloth sized onto the walls. Like the Edwards residence, the Lang house has a carriage entrance from St. Clair Avenue. All three of these houses have simple dormers set into a wide facia above the cornice. The facades of the White and Lang homes have heavy pilasters at the corners with elaborate Corinthian caps supporting the cornice. When the Langs lived in the house, there was a beautiful garden on the east side, where annuals were continually changed with the seasons.

Lang and Company was a very successful

wholesale grocery house on Front Street, owned by the brothers Max and Isador Lang. Max Lang and his five sons, some already married, lived in a large Victorian monstrosity at the corner of Northwest Twentieth Avenue and Irving Street. That house was destroyed in a spectacular fire that the neighborhood remembered for years. The Hubbard house (discussed at the front of the book) was later built on the same site. The five sons of Max Lang (Henry, Isador, Julius, Louis, and Edward) had this handsome residence designed and erected as a gift to their parents for their fiftieth wedding anniversary, and indeed, the Langs celebrated their sixtieth anniversary there before both died in 1918.

Son and daughter-in-law Louis and Grace Lang lived in the house for many years.

The Richard Koehler Residence
Northwest Nineteenth Avenue at
the corner of Johnson Street

RICHARD KOEHLER was born in Frankfurt, Germany, and educated at the University of Karlsruhe; technical training led him into operational and constructional work on the German railroads. British and German bond holders financed the old Oregon and California Railroad. To watch their interests, Koehler was sent to Portland as a special agent. When that railroad was absorbed by national interests, he became the purchasing agent on both the Southern Pacific and the Northern Pacific lines.

The Koehlers' large house was designed with a center hall like many of the Whidden and Lewis plans, but it was much grander in size and finish than most; the detailing was as fine as that on any house in Portland at the time. Like the other large houses on Nineteenth Avenue from Everett to Lovejoy streets, it occupied a half-block. The architects used a new approach here. A flat roof was raised on a wide facia over the cornice, and attic windows were placed in the facia. The superfluous railing above these windows has

been gone for many years and really is not missed. The terrace with the baluster rail in front was repeated across the rear of the house. It commanded a lovely garden that was shut off from Eighteenth Avenue by a high laurel hedge.

The house is still standing in good repair, although the Victorian Gothic mansions of the Couch families that surrounded it have been gone for years; only the Ayer house across the street remains a companion. Not so long ago a heavy snowstorm stopped the traffic for a day. Once again, the two old houses rested in the quietness of bygone years.

At the turn of the century, the Northwest area, or Nob Hill as it was called, was characterized by broad-leaved shade trees along the streets and comfortable domesticity in the dwellings. The lush gardens thrived as a result of Portland's damp climate. There were no automobiles or traffic noises, just streets graded with dirt and wooden crossings to ward off the mud.

The Elmer E. Lytle Residence
Northwest Twenty-Fourth Avenue at Johnson Street

THE ELABORATE CENTER DORMER, the great bay window on the Johnson Street side, and the bow windows on either side of the south chimney are delightful innovative details of this dignified house, which was the Lytle family home for many years. Elmer Lytle was a wealthy mine and railroad owner who removed his family in later years to an even larger house in Irvington. When the Lytles left, the property became a dormitory for the Hill Military Academy. As the Academy lacked a parade ground, Twenty-Fourth Avenue and the side streets resounded to marching feet for many years. When the Hill family moved their school to Rocky Butte, the Lytle house suffered the fate of so many of these large mansions; slow deterioration as a rooming house and then demolition.

The Joseph A. Sladen Residence
2210 Northwest Flanders Street

WILLIAM WHIDDEN'S SON TOM told me once that Ion Lewis did most of the firm's residential designing. True or not, this house certainly reflects Lewis' Boston background. It would be perfectly at home in Milton, Newton, Brookline, or any other turn-of-the-century Boston suburb. Boston architectural offices filled those towns with houses having the same excellent proportions and style as this one. Many are still fine homes.

For the Sladen house Whidden and Lewis developed a new plan for their Colonial Revival facades. The entrance is set quite close to the street to allow for an expansive lawn in the rear. The living room and dining rooms face this rear lawn with a long porch opening off the living room. An important stairway to the right of the front door rises up beside a long leaded-glass window. A library is to the left of the front door; the service area is in the right wing by itself. It is a workable and admirable plan.

Long ago, the austere white dwelling with the contrasting black shutters was a classic New England gift to Portland, but the house has been divided into apartments and these days looks old and tired.

The William Sargent Ladd Residence
11175 Southwest Riverwood Road

WILLIAM S. LADD was born in Portland and educated at Andover and Amherst. He was president of the Ladd and Tilton Bank and the head of a family that held great land sections of Portland, including Eastmoreland, Ladd's Addition, Laurelhurst, and Dunthorpe. With his many civic duties, Ladd at one time was probably the most prominent man in the city.

19

He developed this country place as a summer residence where the family could escape the heat of the city (though Portland had little heat to run from). The Ladds had a strange habit of exchanging houses and seldom selling. After a few years the Charles Ladds took over the place from the William Ladds and made it a year-around home. Through the First World War the Corbetts (cousins) lived here to be near the Red Electric trains to the city.

Only by going inside does one realize how enormous this house is. There are beautifully proportioned fireplaces, fine moldings and cornices, and one of Whidden and Lewis' most elegant stairways. Like all of the firm's houses, this one is very livable. A wide entrance hall runs the length of the house; in the rear an imposing stairway rises beside a group of Palladian windows. The dining room is to the right of the stairs, and in the front corner is a paneled library. Windows in the large drawing room to the left of the hall overlook the river and the south garden.

In 1920, the house was purchased by Guy Talbot, the president of Pacific Power and Light Company. The Talbot family removed the porch across the front and assembled the present entrance from the original columns and rail of the porch. The place still stands on high ground looking across the river to the Waverley Country Club. It remains a private home and is kept in perfect order.

The Philip Buehner Residence
5511 Southeast Hawthorne Boulevard

THIS SITE was once the overnight stop for the stagecoach journey between Vancouver and Oregon City (a trip that takes thirty minutes by car today), and when the Buehners bought the place an inn stood on the property. The family intended to remodel and enlarge the inn, but when they discovered dry rot they had it demolished. Whidden and Lewis designed this imposing mansion to replace the stage stop.

The dominant two-story porte cochere of the house is centered at the end of Hawthorne Boulevard. Before trees and telephone wires appeared, one could see this facade from a distance of two miles. Indeed, the exterior of the house is beautifully detailed. An interesting pergola to the south and east of the house once opened onto elaborate gardens.

Today a college keeps the house in excellent order for its administration offices.

The Sigmund Frank Residence
Southwest Twelfth Avenue at Clay Street

WHEN SIGMUND FRANK arrived in Portland from Germany in 1872, he found work as a clerk in a dry-goods store that a fellow countryman, Aaron Meier, had established earlier. Frank became Meier's business partner a few years after that, and later he married Meier's eldest daughter. The rest of the story of the Meier and Frank department store is well known.

The Franks built this house in 1893 and lived here with their two sons, Lloyd and Aaron. It was a beautiful house as long as the family occupied it. Its siding was painted a warm gray, the trim an off-white, and the shutters a very dark green. It is an excellent example of how very adept Whidden and Lewis were at the development of the Colonial Revival. The only photograph extant—too poor to be reproduced here—shows the house in its prime, with its graceful rounded porch to one side and the "matching" garage to hold, of all things, two cars.

It is interesting to note how much variation there was in design among the Whidden and Lewis houses that have entrances with two-story porticos. This beautifully proportioned ex-

21

ample of that design supports the second-floor balcony with a delicate wrought-iron railing. With all this grandeur, it is disappointing to find the insignificant front door tucked into one corner in an effort to provide light on the landing of a baronial staircase behind the portico.

Over the decades, the residences in the neighborhood changed from houses to tall apartment buildings, and in the early 1950s, this house was destroyed to make way for a high-rise.

The William MacMaster Residence
1041 Southwest Vista Avenue

IT IS HARD TO BELIEVE that this pleasant Colonial house on Vista Avenue, now facing the Vista St. Clair Apartments, was at one time a great Victorian mansion with the narrow end facing the street. When Whidden and Lewis remodeled the place, they turned it so that the side faced Vista Avenue, and they added the two-story colonnade. The Victorian excesses were removed and a Colonial Revival design emerged. The balcony over the entrance and the dormers at the attic are fine features. The main rooms at the rear face the gardens that at one time ran up to the street behind the house.

The MacMaster family commissioned the remodeling, and members of that family lived here for many years. The house, which is still a private residence, is best seen from Main Street.

The Leopold Hirsch Residence
1115 Southwest King Avenue

ODDLY, ALL THE GRAND HOUSES on King Avenue were crowded onto tiny pieces of property. This one, for example, is wedged onto a fifty-square-foot lot. The heavy portico is an excellent example of classic architecture but is too dominant for the plain house behind it; also, the way in which the portico creates a porch-on-porch effect across the front is not very successful. Neverthe-

22

less, the place has a pleasant domestic quality. It is thought that Alfred Holman built this house and never lived in it. It has always been kept a private residence.

The Dr. William Jones Residence
Northwest Flanders Street at the corner of Twenty-Third Avenue

ALL THE HOUSES discussed in this treatise were built during a time in which imposing dwellings were regarded as symbols of achievement. A large house on an open corner reflected social prominence and monetary success. There was no better way to show the importance of a residence (and its occupants) than to have a great two-story colonnade at the entrance. (Good examples of this are Buckingham Palace and the White House.)

The colonnade on the Jones house seems to be the only circular colonnade Whidden and Lewis designed, and it is executed in perfect proportions. The house's gambrel roof is attractive; unlike other such roofs shown in this book, it does not make the building seem top-heavy. The circular window heads of the unusual dormers echo the round roof of the colonnade. The pleasant large bay on the side was at the end of the library; a drawing room was across the center hall. The house has the same balanced windows around the entrance and the same long front ter-

race that the firm used in so many of its Colonial Revival designs.

The house, which was built in 1903, was one of six handsome residences that Whidden and Lewis designed on the two upper blocks of Flanders Street. For many years it was the home of the Ludwig Hirsch family, but it was torn down in the late 1960s.

The Milton Smith Residence
3434 Southwest Kelly Avenue

BECAUSE THIS HOUSE has all the elements of East Coast design, it is often thought to be the work of McKim, Mead and White. In particular, its design is similar to their nationally famous Newport houses. When the house was built, it featured many architectural elements that were new to Portland. At a time when display was popular, it turned its back on the street, showing only a simple but beautifully proportioned facade. Instead of a dominant and highly detailed entrance, the front door was hidden in an inconspicuous corner of the porch; a dormer framed with tall chimneys was another design scheme that hadn't been seen before. The main rooms and a long veranda stretch across the rear, overlooking the sloping gardens and the placid river. Now the gardens are gone and the porch looks out on a freeway, but still a mature dignity overcomes the shabbiness.

Milton Smith, an attorney, was the father of Josephine Andrews, a well-known interior decorator with a refreshing flair that has gone down in Portland history.

Anonymous Residence
Northwest Eighteenth Avenue at Irving Street

THIS HOUSE is an enigma. There is no record of it in the Whidden and Lewis listings, yet it contains all the architectural detailing that the office used in other homes including the classic corner

24

boards, the dentil course at the eaves, the flat bowed bay window, and the elaborate railing over the porch. One new feature is the roof; the gable end was on the main facade, a design that was not used again.

An importer, S. Ban, lived in the house for a short time. It has been gone for many years.

The Richard King Residence
Southwest Twentieth Avenue at Salmon Street

FOR HALF A CENTURY this house's great portico looked over the top of the Multnomah Club to the city beyond, a landmark for the west side of Portland. Nahum King, who built this residence for his son Richard, developed the blocks on "King Hill" into an area of very fine homes, many of which are still standing. Whidden and Lewis used all the earmarks of the Classic Revival style to make the residence an imposing edifice. This view is from the Salmon Street hill; the back of the house ran along Twenty-First Avenue. Today the site is occupied by the many-storied Portland Towers.

The C. E. S. Wood Residence
Southwest Vista Avenue and King's Court

CHARLES ERSKINE SCOTT WOOD was one of early Portland's most colorful characters. He was a creative writer of prose and poetry, an accomplished artist, a career soldier, a practicing attor-

25

ney, a sophisticated bon vivant, and a dedicated, though non-conforming, citizen. An 1874 graduate of the United States Military Academy at West Point, he came west with the army and was stationed at the Vancouver barracks. From there, he took part in the Nez Percé War and the Bannock Indian Wars, but eventually he resigned his commission in a show of compassion for Chief Joseph and his people, whom the government had banned from the Wallowa Mountains and forced onto a reservation.

In 1883 Portland became Wood's home. He settled into a law practice and over the years became an expert in corporate and maritime law. His life here was filled with civic duties. He helped found the original library and art museum; it is likely that through him, Whidden and Lewis were given the contracts for those buildings. When the Skidmore Fountain was planned, Woods arranged for his friend Olin Warner to do the design and sculpture, and he wrote the expression for the plaque on the basin: "Good citizens are the riches of a city."

Childe Hassam, J. Alden Weir, and Albert Pinkham Ryder, all painters in the American Impressionist school, were close friends and constant visitors of Wood's. (The first painting ever acquired by the city art museum is a Hassam oil of Mt. Hood painted from the Wood residence second-floor balcony. In later years, the Ryder, Weir, and Hassam paintings that Portland families acquired attracted buyers from New York galleries, who trekked west to bid for them.)

In 1895 Wood and his wife, Nannie Mole Smith, built this residence on a half block of King Hill. The house, which was set quite close to the street, had a view of the city and the mountains. Five children grew up in the house, which over the years was filled with antiques and treasures of art.

No one in the present Wood family has a picture of the house's exterior, and none seems to exist, but the garden view shown here hints of the house's Colonial Revival style. I remember the facade, which was centered with a paneled doorway and side lights at street level. A small porch with a lattice rail above the door had a Palladian window part way to the second floor. The house had a high hipped roof with one good-sized Colonial dormer and very tall chimneys. There was a porch at the rear, which extended the entire length of the house. Steps led down to terraces held by stone walls with classic balustrades. The view from the porch to the gardens in bloom must have been impressive.

After Mr. and Mrs. Wood died, the property was given as a gift to the Portland Garden Club. The house was torn down and a clubhouse was erected on some of the foundations. Over the years, club members have maintained and developed the gardens, which today are a Portland showcase.

The Dr. Holt Wilson Residence
Northwest Nineteenth Avenue and Everett Street

CAPTAIN JOHN COUCH, who developed his land claim into the residential area of Northwest Portland, had an unusually large number of affluent grandchildren. I can think of twelve or fourteen splendid houses that they built for themselves at the turn of the century and in the decade that followed. Strangely enough, this house and the original Abbot Mills house are the only two that were designed by Whidden and Lewis.

This house, which stood across the street from Trinity Church, has been gone for many years. There are no good photographs of it, although I have put together a drawing of the facade from some faded snapshots. The house was designed early (1892), and many of its features were repeated in other Whidden and Lewis Colonial Revival designs. The handsome dormer with its broken pediment appears again in the James Honeyman house. The heavy wood quoins at the exterior corners are on the Russell, the Therkelsen, and the Koehler houses. The pil-

lared entrance porch with terraces on either side shows up repeatedly. The firm used favorite design elements again and again but disguised them slightly with fresh facades.

The pointed sash of the French doors to the left of the entrance is a jarring feature. As a youngster watching from the streetcar I wondered why such a nice house had such strange windows. I still wonder. Neither Whidden nor Lewis was fond of flamboyant design, so I suspect the effect was requested by the client.

THE QUEEN ANNE STYLE

THE TERM *Queen Anne* applied to domestic architecture can cover many delightful designs and many sins. In Portland we think of shingled houses on the east side, some with towers and bays and others with a roof over the front porch, swooping up to the third floor. Webster defines Queen Anne as "a style of architecture characterized by imitation of English vernacular work of the late seventeenth century, often with an eclectic mixture of medieval, eighteenth century, and Japanese motifs." This gives us a broad field in which to work. Vincent Scully in his book *American Architecture and Urbanism* ignores that definition, yet he describes aptly how the residential design of the nineteenth century reached out to European forms to dramatize the picturesque.

The history of the style dates back to the reign of Queen Anne and the four Georges, when a Dutch influence on domestic design was gradually Anglicized. The increasing middle class demanded convenient and comfortable houses. At the beginning of the nineteenth century a spirit of revolt spread through Europe, unraveling stereotyped social conventions and traditions and reviving past styles. The Revival occurred in the late nineteenth century, with a similar revolt against the stifling atmosphere of the Victorian era. Private houses in the United States became an inflated collection of medieval and classic parts borrowed from Tudor, Georgian, Classic, and Federal styles.

The most successful and influential architect of the Queen Anne Revival was an Englishman, Richard Norman Shaw, who practiced from approximately 1870 to 1910. His designs covered the architectural spectrum from London banks, Scotland Yard, and rural churches, to the town houses and fine country residences that made him famous. Shaw's materials were more varied than had been seen before, and his designs had a highly personal touch and a genuine finesse. Although he used all the former styles, as did others at this time, Shaw combined them to create an individualistic design that brought on a flood of imitation from his contemporaries. An example of his work that had great influence is the Old Swan House in London, a private mansion overlooking the Thames from the Chelsea Embankment. The symmetrical fenestration of the upper stories is in the style of the early eighteenth century, but these upper stories are cantilevered out in a most picturesque manner. The pleasant oriel windows of the second floor, with curved leaded glass and decorative pargeting beneath the sills, are lifted from the romantic period. The Old Swan House illustrates well the basis of the Queen Anne Revival: older architectural styles blended to create rich extravaganzas.

The George Good Residence
Northwest Nineteenth Avenue at Kearney Street

THIS HOUSE, built in 1892, shared a half-block with the second house of W. B. Ayer, and the two buildings complemented each other in design and taste. The Queen Anne style shows here in all its facets. The stucco double gabel with paneling between the windows is very typical of Shaw's houses, as is the downspout in the center of the panel. The main body of the house was of a tawny-colored, odd-sized brick brought from England—probably as ballast in grain ships. There was a combination of casement and double-hung windows painted white, again typical of the style. A sweeping drive that came in from Nineteenth Avenue and went out to Kearney Street gave the house the air of a grand mansion. It has since been remodeled beyond recognition.

George Good, the president of the Bank of British Columbia, was the son-in-law of Cicero Hunt Lewis, an early Portland entrepreneur.

The Winslow B. Ayer Residence
811 Northwest Nineteenth Avenue

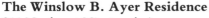

TOGETHER, the Winslow B. Ayer residence and the George Good house made a handsome block between Johnson and Kearney streets. The Ayer house embodies the Queen Anne Revival at its very best, and many consider it Whidden and Lewis' finest residential work. There is balance in the facade, and yet the plan is open. A large living room extends from the center hall, with a library behind it, and at one time a brick-walled cutting garden was off the library. The windows of the library are diamond-paned, but the others in the house are double hung—a Queen Anne touch. The arched loggia to the side of the front door is actually a gallery leading from the driveway to the front entrance. Behind this gallery is the dining room, with a shallow oval bay. This residence has a comfortable, domestic character,

but it might have been austere and forbidding in less competent hands.

Winslow B. Ayer was an active participant in Portland city affairs. The gifts that he and Mrs. Ayer left to the Oregon Art Institute and the Multnomah County Library Association are testimonies to their great generosity and their exceptional taste.

The Ayer residence now houses corporate offices and is kept in excellent condition.

The Herbert Holman Residence
2359 Northwest Overton Street

WHEN PORTLANDERS THINK of Queen Anne style, many probably envision designs similar to the Holman house; numerous shingled houses more flamboyant than this appear throughout the city. The plan features a basic center-hall Colonial design, but no Colonial Revival house would sport such a delightful center section. The entrance porch is a half oval, which supports a second-floor balcony circling a half-oval bay. This balcony, in turn, supports a third-floor balcony, fronting a heavy gabel end. This design element could have been a disaster, but here it is a well-balanced focal point. The combination of siding on the first floor and shingles on the second is another characteristic of the Queen Anne style.

The house is still standing.

34

The Zera Snow Residence
*Northwest Twentieth Avenue at
the corner of Johnson Street*

THE DESIGN of the Snow house harks back to the work of McKim, Mead and White. Indeed, the same design and detailing can be seen in several of the large "cottages" that the firm built at Newport. The Snow house was one of the early Whidden and Lewis projects and an important assignment for the firm. It is an English approach to the Queen Anne style, with an interesting off-center entrance and a combination of various exterior materials. The upper floor was stained shingles and the lower floor small bricks, the same color as those on the George Good house, indeed probably from the same ballast shipment (both houses were under construction in 1891).

As with other Whidden and Lewis mansions, no expense was spared. There were imported marble fireplaces, fine plaster moldings on the ceilings, and exotic wood paneling. The house, which turned its back on the street like a London town house, was set almost on the sidewalk. A vestibule led up a few steps to a great hall, another bit of design borrowed from the English. The hall was beautifully paneled; a fireplace was on one side and an imposing stairway rose from the corner of the room. The drawing room, which faced out onto the garden, featured a half-circle design; one can see from the plan what a handsome room it was. The most unusual part of the design, the oval dining room, also looked out on the garden and, like other rooms in the house, was paneled in cherry. The exceptional fireplace was done in Carrara marble with a carved mantel of the same cherry as the paneling. The bow-shaped den (or library) at the front of the house featured bookcases built under a row of high windows. Upstairs there were four large bedrooms and three baths with the usual servants' quarters. Despite its dimensions, this was a pleasant, livable family residence.

Zera Snow was a successful attorney. A few

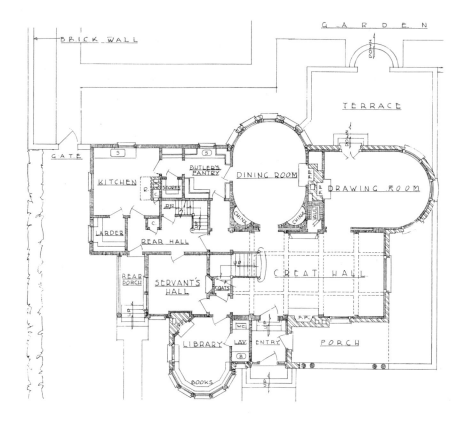

years after building this house, he sold it to the Shevlin family, whose timber mill in Bend was well known. They lived in the house most of its lifetime and were responsible for developing the walled garden that stretched halfway down to Nineteenth Avenue. Later the place became a boarding house, but it deteriorated and finally was torn down in the 1950s.

THE RICHARDSONIAN ROMANESQUE: BRUTAL ARCHITECTURE IN STONE

A T THE END of the American Civil War, architecture in this country was hardly architecture at all but instead was a sinister Victorian effort that reflected the brazen administration of General Grant. That is, in the mid-nineteenth century there was a tendency to develop elaborate designs, then execute them shoddily in whatever material was cheapest, sometimes using paint and stucco to cover construction deficiency.

At about that time, an architect named Henry Hobson Richardson started a practice in New York and set to work reforming the field. Indeed, Richardson not only rejuvenated architecture but dominated it. H. H. Richardson (as he was known) was born in St. James, Louisiana in 1838, and educated at Harvard University and the École des Beaux Arts in Paris. The Harvard education was in mathematics and engineering, which accounts for the precise simplification of his work. Architecture came later in Paris.

Richardson's work is dominated by the principle of spatial continuity, in which a building is a shell containing a volume of space through which continuity flows. His unique designs connected windows horizontally rather than vertically, suppressed and stretched dormers, and made facades that bulged out into curving bays, with the entire volume contained in a continuous envelope of wall and roof planes. He liked to treat his entrances as caverns in a wall of unimaginable thickness, sometimes set in deep, rounded side walls. His buildings had cylindrical towers and vast panels of windows, all brought into one envelope and developed in the earthiness of plain materials.

Richardson's buildings of any size gave the impression that they could swallow up people and vehicles. They were archetypes of stability, characterized by a sense of space combined with mass. Followers of Richardson used the word *engulfment* to describe his heavy arches and rows of deep revealed windows, but his buildings were as geometrically ordered as any by the Georgian masters, and they embodied an American Classicism as well. Thus they combined qualities considered to be opposites: Classicism and Romanticism.

Architects were intrigued with this new theory of systematizing and clarifying designs. They liked the open spaces and the way in which everything flowed together in a horizontal manner. The houses in this chapter are excellent examples of how adept Whidden and Lewis were at handling Richardson's theory.

The William Honeyman Residence
901 Southwest King Avenue

THIS HOUSE, which stood where the King Tower is now, embodies all the features that Richardson put into his residential work. There are the deep-set windows, the romantic tower, the steep pitched roof, and the fanciful dormers. The unfortunate porch across the front darkened both a white-paneled drawing room, very French in character, and a reception room in the round tower. These rooms opened from an entrance hall with a great Jacobean staircase that rose to the flank of windows over the entrance vestibule. The side entrance of this house was a deep-set doorway under a row of tall windows, a design that Richardson implemented so well. A driveway swept up from the street to the entrance and continued on to the rear. This, the Wilcox, the MacKenzie, and the Corbett residences were all built of Tenino stone quarried near Olympia, Washington.

The Dr. Kenneth A. J. MacKenzie Residence
615 Northwest Twentieth Avenue

COMPARE THE PHOTOGRAPH of the MacKenzie residence with the sketch of the Gatwick house at the beginning of this chapter. In both, there are the heavy dark archways, the tower jutting out from the front, the steep roof, and the lack of any formality. In classic Richardsonian style, this building could almost engulf you. All the Romanticism is here, from the bow-windowed dormers and the slits borrowed from castle fortifications, to the heavy stone lintels.

Here is the ideal unbalanced, open plan. The main entrance, placed to the side, opens into a long, oak-paneled hall with a limestone fireplace and an elaborate stairway. The living room is in the front bay with a library behind it. There is a wealth of carving, detailing, and fine ironwork, both in the interior and on the exterior.

41

Dr. MacKenzie was a Canadian who brought to Portland his European medical training. A tireless organizer, he was one of a group that formed the University of Oregon Medical School. After his death, his son-in-law, Roderick Macleay, and his family lived here for many years. The house now belongs to the Episcopal Diocese of Oregon and is used for social services. It is in excellent condition and is well worth a visit.

The Theodore B. Wilcox Residence
931 Southwest King Avenue

FOUR GREAT HOUSES faced King Avenue between Park Place and Yamhill Street; three of them were the designs of Whidden and Lewis. On the corner of Yamhill Street was the Adolph Wolfe home, and next door to the south was the William Honeyman house. A very early Victorian house belonging to the Schuylers (not designed by the firm) was the third, and on the corner was this house, the Wilcox residence. Typically Richardsonian, there is a marked contrast between this house and the Corbett house (discussed next). The stonework with the tall windows is quite the same, but the second floor shingling is much simpler here. Richardson's dark, yawning openings are here, but a dominant bay dwarfs the entrance. The double oak doors and the stone carving are beautifully done. Gardens stretched back to St. Clair Avenue in the rear, and across King Avenue was another garden that now belongs to the Town Club.

The Wilcox house drew great interest during the Second World War when it was occupied by Russian purchasing agents. Today it is the headquarters of a broadcasting company and is kept in perfect order.

The Henry Jagger Corbett Residence
Southwest Madison Street and Park Avenue

WHIDDEN AND LEWIS borrowed many of Richardson's design principles for the Corbett residence. They used his tall single windows sunk deep in stonework, the combination of exterior materials including an interesting shingle pattern on the second floor, and the variety of gable ends that make up the front facade.

The exterior of the Corbett house made no attempt to hide its unbalanced plan. Broad steps led up from the drive to a covered porch; the front door was almost in the corner. The large entrance hall was practically a part of the living room. A stairway with an interesting balustrade rose from the rear of this hall and broke at a landing lighted by a tier of stained-glass windows. Off the hall to the right was a small, comfortable library with a terrazzo fireplace. The bookcases were three-quarters height, and the walls above were covered in grass cloth. The same treatment was used in the living room, which had an interesting Greek panel installed above the fireplace; that treasure is now in the city's art museum.

Behind the living room was a small but pleasant dining room. The trim and wainscot was painted white, and the walls, again, were covered with grass cloth. Upstairs were four bedrooms and more than one bath, a luxury at that time. For such a large house, the rooms had an intimate scale and a look of great comfort. As in the Snow house, there was fine paneling, beautiful marble, and fine exterior stonework. A great deal of the beauty of the interior, however, came from the elegant furnishings, the valuable artwork, and the beautiful appointments.

Henry Jagger Corbett lived in this house for a

very short time. Stricken with tuberculosis, he died in Colorado Springs in 1895. Mrs. Corbett took her family home to the Ladd residence on Sixth Avenue and Jefferson Street, where she lived until that house was torn down for the Oregonian building. Her eldest son, Henry Ladd Corbett, brought his family to this house where they lived for many years, until it was razed in the late twenties to make room for the Masonic Temple, which occupies the entire block. Before long, the large houses as far up as Hall Street were demolished as well, and the Park Blocks lost their residential flavor.

COTTAGES AND MANSIONS
IN THE ENGLISH STYLE

A S I WAS MAKING THE DRAWING of the William Nunn house, it occurred to me how typical that residence was of the English style. It also struck me how very versatile Whidden and Lewis were in all the styles they used, a talent that came from training, ability, and lastly taste, which prevented them from duplicating the cute and darling English cottages that sprung up in Portland neighborhoods after the First World War.

Wealth usually accompanies a Romantic period. John Russell Pope and Harrie Lindeberg designed great mansions along the Eastern Seaboard in a style borrowed from lovely English manor houses, with half timbers, steep roofs, divided window panes, and fine, warm brickwork. Whidden and Lewis did well with this style, although they were among the first to use it locally.

The William H. Nunn Residence
852 Southwest Twenty-First Avenue

HAD THIS HOUSE been built in another neighborhood, it might still be a pleasant private home; few of the Whidden and Lewis houses have as distinct a domestic quality as this one. The pleasant hooded doorway, the small casement windows, and the stained shingles all give an air of comfort and good living. Unfortunately, though, the location was wrong from the start. Multnomah Stadium rose suddenly against the rear garden, breaking the view, and garages marched up the street from Burnside Street almost to the door.

Phillip Jackson, editor of the *Oregon Journal*, and his family lived here for many years. Not long ago the house was nicely refurbished for offices.

The Frank Warren Residence
929 Southwest St. Clair Avenue

THIS GREAT HOUSE, which stood on the northwest corner of St. Clair Avenue and Park Place, had a spectacular view of the city when it was built in 1902. It is not, however, one of the most successful Whidden and Lewis designs. In an attempt to be imposing, they created a top-heavy, overbearing effect. The great half-timbered gable ends and the heavy dormers throw the facade off-scale. Perhaps the error was in placing the front so high above the street.

The wealth of fine millwork, cornices, paneling, and carving in this house was unusual. The fireplaces were remarkable in their detailing, and the cabinet work in the dining room was another example of exceptional craftsmanship. Especially interesting was the great cove at the dining-room ceiling, which surely must have been the pride of the carpenter who installed it.

Despite its size, this probably was a very comfortable house. Mr. Warren was on the *Titanic* when it sank in 1912, but the family continued to

48

live here for many years after his death. The house has since been replaced by a tall apartment tower.

The Isaac N. Lipman Residence
2166 Southwest Yamhill Street

THE LIPMAN HOUSE and the Adolfe Wolfe house (discussed later in this chapter) were built at the same time for the heads of the Lipman, Wolfe department store. Though the two houses share great similarities, this one has a simpler design with almost the quality of an eastern town house. It was recently converted into flats, but its domestic feeling was preserved.

The Henry A. Sargent Residence
2448 NW Johnson Street

THIS PLEASANT HOUSE has all the attributes of the Nunn house discussed at the beginning of the chapter. Whidden and Lewis were very good at achieving fine living qualities when they used this English shingle style. The house has changed little since it was built eighty years ago; it even has the same stained shingles and cream-colored trim. No matter what style of architecture is used, simplicity is the lasting quality.

Henry Sargent was the vice-president of a New England company that made saws for the lumber industry. A few years after the First World War he had the architect Morris White-

49

house design a large house on Portland Heights. Although the client changed designers, the new house has a great deal of the character and detail of this one.

The Adolphe Wolfe Residence
Southwest King Avenue and Yamhill Street

ADOLPHE WOLFE, the founder of the Lipman, Wolfe department store, built this house in 1900 as his family home. The heavy, half-timbered gable ends gave it a formidable feeling, yet the facade had the same balance Whidden and Lewis used in their Classic Revival houses, and the plan was similarly balanced. Even when Whidden and Lewis explored a new style, they did not stray far from the formal plan that runs through all their domestic work. A covered entrance porch with the usual side terraces opened to an L-shaped hall; a monumental staircase rose against great windows on Yamhill Street. There was a dining room to the right of the entrance, a living room to the left, and a library behind.

The house stood vacant for a long time in the 1940s, and after marauders ransacked the place, it was finally torn down.

50

The carriage entrance of the Honeyman house can be seen on the left-hand side of the picture.

The Frank E. Hart Residence
1942 Southwest Montgomery Drive

HERE ONCE AGAIN is a well-kept private home in an elegant neighborhood. It is a large, half-timbered house that turns its entrance to the side, off the driveway that carries through to a lane behind. Whidden and Lewis achieved more of a comfortable domesticity here than in many of their previous houses.

One of the fondest memories in this neighborhood was of Mrs. Hart's Toledo Electric, which somehow always managed the hill up to Portland Heights.

THE ITALIAN VILLA IN OREGON

THE RENAISSANCE of Classic architecture began in Florence, Italy in the early fifteenth century and spread westward through the countries of Europe. It was a rejuvenation of the Greek and Roman styles of architecture. Venice, Rome, and Florence were municipalities that had been transformed into states or republics. Florence became immensely wealthy and was a center of artistic development. The great palazzi such as the Riccardi and the Strozzi were too urban and formidable to have much of an effect on the nineteenth-century domestic architecture, but they served as a fine influence on such American design as banks and municipal buildings. It was the lovely villas that the Florentines built in the hills above Florence at Settignano and Fiesole that gave an "Italian style" to American domestic work. The one I have sketched has the flat roofs, the walled gardens, and the open loggia to view the Arno valley, like many of the villas that are strung through the hills. They are quite large, with beautiful formal gardens, but in spite of their size, they have the first real domestic quality that we find in European dwellings.

The Walter F. Burrell Residence
2610 Southeast Hawthorne Boulevard

IN THIS RESIDENCE, Whidden and Lewis adapted the design of an Italian villa to local needs and climate. The Florentine villa that I sketched for this chapter would not fit into a site on Hawthorne Boulevard, but one can see great similarities between it and the Burrell house; both have flat roofs, numerous tall chimneys, broad eaves, and stucco walls. The delightful third-floor loggia has also been reproduced. Instead of the narrow shuttered windows, Whidden and Lewis used broad undivided panes of glass to light the rooms.

At one time this imposing mansion was surrounded by many acres, and it had a sweeping view of the west side of the city. Later, the area was divided into city blocks and developed into a section called Murrymead. Still, two city blocks surround the house today. The place is now a mortuary, with scarcely a change since it was a private residence. The main rooms, which face south for the view, are now used for services, and their fine proportions and beautiful ornamental plaster work have been maintained. The grounds around the place are kept in pristine order, although the planting has flourished over the years, obstructing the view and hiding the house from the boulevard.

A STUDIED SIMPLICITY
FOR THE NORTHWEST

HOW OFTEN have we in Portland seen the prototype of the house on the opposite page? Various versions of it line the streets of Irvington and Laurelhurst, but the style is not limited to those areas. It evolved at the turn of the century by Americans tired of the elaborate frills of the Victorian age. Because that was also the time of Portland's tremendous growth, the style was used often in this city. A craftsman group in the East produced furniture and house-plan books that featured simplicity and comfort. They had a tremendous effect on middle-class living standards and served as the basis for this plain, almost austere type of dwelling.

The Charles Francis Adams Residence
2363 Northwest Flanders Street

WHIDDEN AND LEWIS designed this house in 1904 for Charles Adams, the president of the United States National Bank of Oregon. Almost stark in its simplicity, it gives a feeling of foursquare honesty. There are brick keystones over the windows, a pierced brick railing on the porch, and brick quoins on the building corners, but because all were constructed of the same material they scarcely can be distinguished. The Adams house is now used for medical offices.

On the right side of this picture is the interesting gable end of the Nunn house.

The Robert L. Sabin Residence
2130 Northeast Twenty-Third Avenue

THIS SIMPLE HOUSE in the heart of Irvington is turned from the street to give the principal rooms a view of the lawn and garden. The excellent proportions of windows and roof line make ornamentation unnecessary.

The James H. Page Residence
Southwest Vista Avenue and Jackson Street

IT TOOK PIONEER SPIRITS to build a house on Portland Heights in 1892, the year the Pages constructed this place. A cable car ran from Jefferson

Street up to Spring Street, but the only other access from the city below was by horse and buggy up the winding Montgomery Drive. Surprisingly, many fine houses were built there despite the difficult access. This house was built much earlier than others included in this chapter, but its square simplicity put it ahead of its time. The three-story tower with its wraparound porch was dubbed the "steamboat style," and one can easily see why.

The driveway came in from Vista Avenue, curving in front of the terrace and the main entrance. From there, a sweeping view of rivers and mountains to the north may have made the isolation worthwhile. The house occupied a half-block facing Jackson Street and backing against Clifton Street. One of the Page children later had a similar house built on the rest of the block, but both houses are gone.

The Henry W. Corbett Summer Residence
Seaview, Washington

IN THE 1880s AND 1890s a train served the Washington beaches from Ilwaco, where passengers on stern-wheelers from Portland disembarked. Henry Winslow Corbett built this house in 1892, when even carriages and horses were shipped on the steamers. This was one of eight or ten large "cottages" that lined the ocean front from Holman Road to Seaview. It is still standing near the station, just down from the famous Shelburne Inn.

The William Whidden Residence
Southwest Military Lane

AT LAST WE COME to that most interesting occurrence in the field of domestic architecture, a house that an architect designed for himself. Here Whidden created a large, comfortable home for a growing family in a beautiful garden setting. Though the exterior is Italian in feeling,

59

it is almost modern in its simplicity. The stucco walls are broken only by a heavy band under the second-story windows, and the very wide eaves that taper from the pitch of the roof cover all the breaks in the facade, making it one unit. For a country house, it has a very formal plan. A center hall runs through the first floor to the staircase, with a drawing room on one side and a sitting room on the other. A library is behind the drawing room, and behind the sitting room is the dining room.

The house was sold just before the First World War to Thomas Kerr, and members of his family lived there for years. In the late 1940s the Kerrs had Thornton Ladd of Pasadena extensively remodel the interior. He built a court at the rear of the house, which created a new entrance to the main hall. The former front entrance became the access to the elaborate gardens that stretched for several acres. Over the years these gardens have matured in beauty, and the house has become a Portland showplace.

The Frank Knapp Residence
2447 Northwest Kearney Street

The Morton Insley Residence

2453 Northwest Kearney Street

THESE TWO SIMPLE HOUSES stood side by side at the head of Kearney Street. They were built for members of the Brazee family, pioneers of the 1840s who built the first portage railroad around the rapids at Cascade Locks. The Brazees operated that railroad for many years until the Oregon Navigation Company took it over. Both houses have been gone for many years.

The George Lawrence Residence

*Northwest Twenty-Third Avenue at
the corner of Flanders Street*

THE GEORGE LAWRENCE COMPANY was established in 1857 to sell harnesses and saddlery, and until it was sold in 1985, it was one of the oldest firms in the city to be still in the hands of the original family. Whidden and Lewis designed a building for the company in 1902, which still stands at the corner of Southwest First Avenue and Oak Street.

The family home was built in 1896. Like the downtown building, it is stark in its simplicity. It looks like what it is: a big, comfortable dwelling. Its only bit of design is the strange splay in the roof as it descends to the gutter line. The landscaping of so many houses of this era seemed to be an afterthought, but here it was excellent.

61

The house at the rear of the photograph is one that Whidden and Lewis designed for the Jacobs family. It is now occupied by the Metropolitan Family Services.

The James McIntosh Wood Residence
Southwest Prospect Drive

THIS HOUSE, built in 1910, was probably the last residential work done by Whidden and Lewis. James Wood, C. E. S. Wood's younger brother, lived only a few years after it was built.

The house is hard by the street with no sidewalk; the street curbing was used for one of the front steps. There is a precipitous drop from the paving; the structure is actually a four-story building in the rear, looking down on the Vista Avenue bridge. Except for the entrance portico, the house lacks any of the ornamentation usually used by Whidden and Lewis. A simpler age had begun.

EPILOGUE

WE HAVE COME through nearly forty years of one architectural practice. Earlier, others in Portland had designed a few large houses, but Whidden and Lewis represented the city's first attempt at a large volume of residential design. It is true that many of these houses were grand mansions belonging to the well-to-do, but architects seldom are asked to do small domestic work.

Manners of living have changed, and now there is little use for these unwieldy mansions. Nevertheless, they represent a period of Portland history, one to which Whidden and Lewis contributed greatly. Their designs always had a dignity of proportion and fine detailing. That is why these are great houses.

Portland, 1989

Index and Inventory of the Residential Architecture of Whidden and Lewis

The architectural office of Sutton and Whitney inherited the drawings and papers of the Whidden and Lewis partnership when the firm went out of business. The listings and comments on the following pages were compiled from those papers. Page numbers are given for those houses discussed in this book.

Buehner, Philip	1908	5511 SE Hawthorne Boulevard	Standing	Well kept as administration offices for the Western Conservative Baptist Seminary.	20
Burrell, Walter F.	1902	2610 SE Hawthorne Boulevard	Standing	Well kept as a mortuary.	54
Clark, George	1900	SE Belmont Street at Fifty-Eighth Avenue	Standing		
Corbett, Henry Jagger		Facing the Park Blocks at SW Madison Street	Demolished	Torn down in 1926 for the present Masonic Temple.	43
Corbett, Henry Winslow	1892	Seaview, Washington	Standing		59
Cox, L. B.	1892	NW Lovejoy Street	Demolished		
Dunlap, C.		SW Sixteenth Avenue at Spring Street	Standing	Built near the top of the old cable car line. Still a private residence.	
Edwards, Henry		SW Main Street at St. Clair Avenue	Standing	Remodeled for offices.	11
Ehrman, Edward	1899	NW Flanders Street	Demolished	Built for the head of Mason, Ehrman, Co., a wholesale grocery concern.	
Frank, Sigmund	1893	SW Twelfth Avenue at Clay Street	Demolished		21
Good, George	1892	NW Nineteenth Avenue at Kearney Street	Standing	Used for offices. Remodeled beyond recognition.	33
Hart, Frank E.	1900	1942 SW Montgomery Drive	Standing	Still a handsome private residence.	51
Hays, H. A.		Aberdeen, Washington	Standing	Built in the heyday of the Grays Harbor lumber boom.	
Hilton, Charles	1898	NW Irving Street near Twenty-Third Avenue	Demolished		
Hirsch, Leopold		1115 SW King Avenue	Standing	Well kept as a private residence.	22

Holman, Herbert		2353 NW Overton Street	Standing	A large Queen Anne house.	34
Honeyman, James D.	1900	864 SW St. Clair Avenue	Standing	Vacant at present. Completely remodeled from an earlier house.	12
Honeyman, William	1893	901 SW King Avenue	Demolished	Now the site of the King Tower.	41
Howe, W. A.		Carlton, Oregon	Demolished		
Hubbard, Russell	1905	NW Twentieth Avenue at Irving Street	Demolished	Now the site of Hubbard House, a group of condominiums.	7
Insley, Morton H.	1906	2353 NW Kearney Street	Demolished	Now the site of the Shaarie Torah Synagogue.	61
Jones, Dr. William	1903	NW Flanders Street at Twenty-Third Avenue	Demolished	Occupied for most of its years by the Ludwig Hirsch family.	23
King, Edward		SW King Avenue at Yamhill Street	Standing	Remodeled beyond recognition.	9
King, Richard		SW Twentieth Avenue at Salmon Street	Demolished	Now the site of the Portland Towers.	25
Knapp, Frank	1906	2447 NW Kearney Street	Demolished	A simple, well-designed house for a widow of the Brazee family.	60
Knapp, Lawrence	1900	NE Hassalo Street at Eighth Avenue	Demolished	One of the fine houses built at the opening of "Holladay Addition."	
Koehler, Richard		NW Nineteenth Avenue at Johnson Street	Standing	Well kept as a group of offices.	17
Ladd, William Mead	1892	Facing the Park Blocks at SW Main Street	Demolished	Extensive alterations to an older, very large Victorian House.	
Ladd, William Sargent	1896	11175 SW Riverwood Road	Standing	Still a very fine private home.	19

69

Ladd Estate, The	1896	SW Tenth Avenue at Clay Street	Demolished	A fine Colonial Revival house built by the Ladds for Dr. Wilson who was headmaster of the Portland Academy.	
Lang, Max M.	1905	2188 SW Park Place	Standing	Well kept as offices.	16
Lawrence, George	1904	NW Flanders Street at Twenty-Third Avenue	Demolished	A large, gray-shingled family home.	61
Lipman, Isaac N.	1900	2166 SW Yamhill Street	Standing	Very well converted into apartments.	49
Lytle, Elmer E.		NW Twenty-Fourth Avenue at Johnson Street	Demolished	Was a dormitory for Hill Military Academy for many years.	18
MacKenzie, Dr. K.A.J.	1902	615 NW Twentieth Avenue	Standing	Now the William Temple House.	41
MacKenzie, W. R.	1902	1131 SW King Avenue	Standing	For many years the Robert Farrell residence. Well kept.	10
MacMaster, William	1895	1041 SW Vista Avenue	Standing	A large Victorian house remodeled by Whidden and Lewis into a Southern Colonial residence.	22
McArthur, Lewis L.	1891	NW Glisan Street	Demolished		
McCamant, Wallace	1899	SW King Avenue at Main Street	Standing	Very well remodeled and brought up to date for a private residence.	10
Mills, Abbot L.	1891	NW Twentieth Avenue at Johnson Street	Demolished	The first Mills house, it was torn down for the large brick residence that stands on the site today.	
Nunn, William H.	1902	852 SW Twenty-First Avenue	Standing	Now a group of offices.	48
Oliphant, D. D.	1891	NE Tillamook Street at Nineteenth Avenue	Standing	Still a private residence.	
Page, James H.	1890	SW Vista Avenue at Jackson Street	Demolished		58

Palmer, E.F.	1891	NW Johnson Street between Twenty-Fourth and Twenty-Fifth avenues	Standing	One of two houses in the middle of the block that have the mark of Whidden and Lewis' work.	
Paul, A. J.	1902	North Williams Avenue	Standing	Hardly recognizable.	
Rush, R. L.	1902	2281 NW Everett Street	Standing	Remodeled for the Metropolitan Family Service headquarters.	
Russell, James M.	1904	1135 SW Vista Avenue	Standing	Well kept private home.	14
Russell & McLeod	1890	NW Marshall Street at Twenty-Fourth Avenue	Standing	A two-story Colonial Revival house built for speculation.	
Sabin, Robert L.	1904	2130 NE Twenty-Third Avenue	Standing	Private residence.	58
Sargent, Henry A.	1903	2448 NW Johnson Street	Standing	Private residence.	49
Shelton, Ada L.	1903	SE Sixteenth Avenue at Washington Street	Standing	A plain, square house devoid of ornamentation.	
Sibson, William S.	1891	SW Military Lane	Demolished	A large Queen Anne country house. For many years the home of Helen Ladd Corbett. Replaced by five well-designed Colonial houses.	
Sladen, Joseph A.	1897	2210 NW Flanders Street	Standing	Remodeled into apartments.	19
Smith, David	1895	Forest Grove, Oregon	No record.		
Smith, Henry E.	1891	Oregon City, Oregon	No record.		
Smith, Milton W.	1898	3434 SW Kelly Street	Standing	In very good condition as physicians' offices.	24
Snow, Zera	1891	NW Twentieth Avenue at Johnson Street	Demolished	Now the site of a large apartment building.	35

Stearns, Loyal B.		SW King Avenue at Yamhill Street	Demolished	A very fine Colonial Revival house with a reverse plan to take advantage of the views.	
Therkelsen, Lauritz W.	1897	SW Eleventh Avenue at Market Street	Demolished	Now part of the Portland State University campus.	15
Trevett, Theodore B.	1890	2347 NW Flanders Street	Standing	In excellent condition.	8
Trimble, W. F.		SW St. Clair Avenue	Demolished	A large gambrel-roofed house at Park Place with a reverse plan for the view of the city.	
Wallace, Lucien W.	1889	NW Flanders Street at Twenty-Fourth Avenue	Standing	Remodeled by Whidden and Lewis into the present house.	5
Warren, Frank M.	1902	929 SW St. Clair Avenue	Demolished	Replaced by high-rise condominiums.	48
Watson, J. Frank	1891	Facing the Park Blocks at SW Hall Street	Demolished	Now part of the Portland State University campus.	13
Whidden, William		SW Military Lane	Standing	Still a very fine country residence.	59
White, Isam	1904	NW Twentieth Avenue at Everett Street	Standing	Well kept as a residence.	15
Wilcox, Theodore B.	1892	931 SW King Avenue	Standing	Beautifully kept as the offices of a broadcasting studio.	42
Wilson, Dr. Holt C.	1892	NW Nineteenth Avenue at Everett Street	Demolished	A large Colonial Revival house, typical of the firm, built for a member of the Couch family.	27
Wolfe, Adolphe	1900	SW King Avenue at Yamhill Street	Demolished	Replaced by a motel.	50
Wood, C. E. S.	1895	SW Vista Avenue at King's Court	Demolished	Probably the firm's most successful Colonial Revival design. The elaborate gardens are now incorporated with the Portland Garden Club building erected on the grounds.	25

Wood, James McIntosh	1909	SW Prospect Drive	Standing	Still a private residence.	62
Owner unknown	1901	Northwest corner of NW Eighteenth Avenue at Irving Street	Demolished		24

ILLUSTRATION CREDITS

COLOPHON

In order to jump the gun on the quincentenary of the introduction of Francesco Griffo's design of the Bembo typeface, an event that book designers should mark in 1995, it was decided to set this book in that fine "old style" typeface. First used in Cardinal Bembo's *De Aetna* in 1495, this influential typeface was later, in 1974, used for Richard Marlitt's other Oregon Historical Society Press book on architecture, *Nineteenth Street*.

The Press' collaborators on this anticipatory celebration have been:
   Irish Setter of Portland for typesetting
   Malloy Lithography of Ann Arbor, Michigan printed (on 70 lb. Spring Forge paper) and bound this volume.

The Oregon Historical Society Press designed and produced *Matters of Proportion*.